Join our email list to get inspirational daily quotes
and the latest and greatest information from the
Gutsy Women Win movement
and to become a part of it:
http://aha.pub/JoinGutsyMovement

Gutsy Leaders

140 Bits of Wisdom on How to Build Great Teams
with Vision and Compassion

Pat Obuchowski

Foreword by
Mitchell Levy, The AHA Guy

THiNKaha®

An Actionable Business Journal

E-mail: info@thinkaha.com
20660 Stevens Creek Blvd., Suite 210
Cupertino, CA 95014

Published by THiNKaha®
20660 Stevens Creek Blvd., Suite 210, Cupertino, CA 95014
http://thinkaha.com
E-mail: info@thinkaha.com

First Printing: February 2018
Hardcover ISBN: 978-1-61699-234-7   1-61699-234-4
Paperback ISBN: 978-1-61699-233-0   1-61699-233-6
eBook ISBN: 978-1-61699-232-3   1-61699-232-8
Place of Publication: Silicon Valley, California, USA
Paperback Library of Congress Number: 2017954567

Trademarks

Warning and Disclaimer

Dedication

I dedicate this book to all who model the heart of leadership and know that all great leaders are servant leaders. I also dedicate this book to my coaching clients and those leaders I meet along this life journey who inspire me to be a better leader and who open their hearts and show a passion for stepping into leading from any seat at the proverbial table. Go Forth. Do Good.

Acknowledgement

I'd like to acknowledge Mitchell Levy, the CEO of THINKaha, and his team, whose publications bring practical wisdom to the world. With their support and vision, this book and many others have provided an opportunity for voices to be heard.

How to Read a THiNKaha® Book
A Note from the Publisher

The THiNKaha series is the CliffsNotes of the 21st century. The value of these books is that they are contextual in nature. Although the actual words won't change, their meaning will change every time you read one as your context will change. Experience your own "AHA!" moments ("AHAmessages™") with a THiNKaha book; AHAmessages are looked at as "actionable" moments—think of a specific project you're working on, an event, a sales deal, a personal issue, etc. and see how the AHAmessages in this book can inspire your own AHAmessages, something that you can specifically act on. Here's how to read one of these books and have it work for you:

1. Read a THiNKaha book (these slim and handy books should only take about 15-20 minutes of your time!) and write down one to three actionable items you thought of while reading it. Each journal-style THiNKaha book is equipped with space for you to write down your notes and thoughts underneath each AHAmessage.

2. Mark your calendar to re-read this book again in 30 days.

3. Repeat step #1 and write down one to three more AHAmessages that grab you this time. I guarantee that they will be different than the first time. BTW: this is also a great time to reflect on the actions taken from the last set of AHAmessages you wrote down.

After reading a THiNKaha book, writing down your AHAmessages, re-reading it, and writing down more AHAmessages, you'll begin to see how these books contextually apply to you. THiNKaha books advocate for continuous, lifelong learning. They will help you transform your ahas into actionable items with tangible results until you no longer have to say "AHA!" to these moments—they'll become part of your daily practice as you continue to grow and learn.

As The AHA Guy at THiNKaha, I definitely practice what I preach. I read 2-3 AHAbooks a month in addition to those that we publish and take away two to three different action items from each of them every time. Please e-mail me your AHAs today!

Mitchell Levy
publisher@thinkaha.com

THiNKaha®

Contents

Foreword by Mitchell Levy 11

Introduction 13

Section I
Focus on You 15

Section II
Gutsy Leaders 39

Section III
Building Other Gutsy Leaders:
All about Your Team 53

Section IV
Be Bold or Go Home 61

Section V
Attitude Wins 83

Section VI
Something Bigger Than You 107

About the Author 117

Foreword

by Mitchell Levy, The AHA Guy at AHAthat and TEDx Speaker

Gutsy leaders are human. They live and act in alignment with their values and with the traits of authenticity, integrity, and trustworthiness. They are fun to hang around and aren't afraid to give feedback to transform and help inspire those around them, and to receive feedback to become better leaders.

Life and business has changed since the agricultural age, a period with a strong hierarchal structure because the farms were run by families. In that economy, we knew how to network because it had a strong barter component at its core. You grew the corn and your neighbors grew the potatoes, while another raised the chickens and cows.

When we transitioned to the industrial economy, we were hammered with efficiency. We kept the hierarchical structure: there was a boss and workers, and they didn't mix. Jobs were structured to be focused, concrete, and routine. With the industrial age, we lost a portion of our ability to network.

We are still in the transition to the internet/social economy. We're relearning how to network. We're relearning how to make jobs fun. We're learning that hierarchical structures don't work and that great ideas come from anywhere. We're also learning that we need to pay attention to the customer, as just one voice can rock the boat.

In the transition to this new paradigm of living and working, we need leaders who will buck the trend that was established in the agricultural and industrial economies and who will focus on the needs of those living in the social economy. These are the gutsy leaders of today, and at some point, these leaders will no longer be called "Gutsy"—they will be called human.

Introduction

I have always been inspired by others' words. I have been sending a "Quote for Your Day" via email and posting to social media for over sixteen years with the hope that these words may motivate and inspire. I truly believe that we never know how we impact others, because every now and then, when I start to think it's a waste of time to post these quotes, I get a message that says, "You have no idea how I needed this today." These personal notes remind me how much each of us needs a little bit of inspiration.

This book and the words I chose are meant to inspire and perhaps motivate you along your life and leadership journey to take some action and do something that makes you feel a bit afraid. As I say, "Feel the GULP and do it anyway." GULP is that scary, exhilarated feeling you get when you start to do something you've never done before. Watch out—it can become addictive . . . and that's a good thing.

These are words that I live by and have found in my business to ring true for the leaders I have the honor to serve.

I hope they ring true for you.

Share the AHA messages from this book socially by going to
http://aha.pub/GutsyLeaders.

Section I

Focus on You

Gutsy Leadership is an inward job. The AHAmessages that follow encourage you to spend time in self-reflection and self-observation, get quiet enough to hear your own answers, and trust in yourself to know you have those answers.

1

Ask yourself: "If I were really gutsy, what would I do?" @Pat_Obuchowski
http://aha.pub/GutsyLeaders

_____

_____

_____

2

If what's stopping you from being a #GutsyLeader is you, get out of your way. Fast. @Pat_Obuchowski

_____

_____

_____

3

You have the answer within you to be a #GutsyLeader. Just get quiet enough to hear it. @Pat_Obuchowski

_____

_____

_____

4

#GutsyLeaders make their life 1st Class. Are you doing that? @Pat_Obuchowski

_____

_____

_____

5

Every day, #GutsyLeaders make the comfort zones that aren't serving them a little bit smaller. @Pat_Obuchowski

_____

_____

_____

6

Every day, #GutsyLeaders consciously decrease the things that are easy to do and don't serve them well. @Pat_Obuchowski

_____

_____

_____

7

#GutsyLeaders find their spontaneity to help their creativity. @Pat_Obuchowski

_____

_____

_____

8

Commit. #GutsyLeaders find that their decisions are a release. @Pat_Obuchowski

_____

_____

_____

9

#GutsyLeaders learn more to earn more
and become masters at what they do.
@Pat_Obuchowski

_____

_____

_____

10

Pay attention to your intention.
#GutsyLeaders focus on the impact of their
actions. @Pat_Obuchowski

_____

_____

_____

11

"Savor it all" is a #GutsyLeader motto.
@Pat_Obuchowski

_____

_____

_____

12

Since emotions are contagious, #GutsyLeaders choose theirs carefully for the greatest impact. @Pat_Obuchowski

_____

_____

_____

13

#GutsyLeaders never get really good at anything they don't want to do. Why bother? @Pat_Obuchowski

_____

_____

_____

14

Find one thing each day to celebrate.
#GutsyLeaders always stop and celebrate
the everyday achievements.
@Pat_Obuchowski

_____

_____

_____

15

Confusion can be clarity. It may be telling you what not to do. #GutsyLeaders know this. @Pat_Obuchowski

_____

_____

_____

16

Find the peaceful place inside you.
#GutsyLeaders visit this place often.
@Pat_Obuchowski

_____

_____

_____

17

#GutsyLeaders know the value of life and
how to meander through it.
@Pat_Obuchowski

_____

_____

_____

18

Be aware of your energy. Minding your mood is always in the consciousness of #GutsyLeaders. @Pat_Obuchowski

_____

_____

_____

19

#GutsyLeaders look for the positive in people -- especially in themselves. What have you seen in others today? @Pat_Obuchowski

_____

_____

_____

20

Be more vulnerable to build more trust. This is a key element of every #GutsyLeader. @Pat_Obuchowski

_____

_____

_____

21

Since #GutsyLeaders have to live with their decisions, they decide for themselves.
@Pat_Obuchowski

_____

_____

_____

22

#GutsyLeaders simply begin. They don't wait for the perfect time or place.
@Pat_Obuchowski

_____

_____

_____

23

#GutsyLeaders don't wait to be chosen to lead. They choose to lead.
@Pat_Obuchowski

_____

_____

_____

24

#GutsyLeaders rest relentlessly.
@Pat_Obuchowski

_____

_____

_____

25

#GutsyLeaders listen like they want to be
listened to: with head and heart.
@Pat_Obuchowski

_____

_____

_____

26

Take time to do something that gives you joy. #GutsyLeaders know the importance of this. @Pat_Obuchowski

_____

_____

_____

27

For #GutsyLeaders, time is their most valuable asset. They invest in it wisely.
@Pat_Obuchowski

_____

_____

_____

28

#GutsyLeaders know how to stop and reset and recover. @Pat_Obuchowski

_____

_____

_____

29

#GutsyLeaders make great memories. @Pat_Obuchowski

_____

_____

_____

30

You know you know, you know?
#GutsyLeaders know they know, you know?
@Pat_Obuchowski

_____

_____

_____

31

#GutsyLeaders know it's not all about them.
They know it's about something bigger.
@Pat_Obuchowski

_____

_____

_____

32

#GutsyLeaders never let anything come between them and the person they want to be. @Pat_Obuchowski

_____

_____

_____

33

Economizing their speech is something #GutsyLeaders are good at. Get to the point. @Pat_Obuchowski

_____

_____

_____

34

Feeling everything that makes you human is what passion is about. #GutsyLeaders know this and practice this. @Pat_Obuchowski

_____

_____

_____

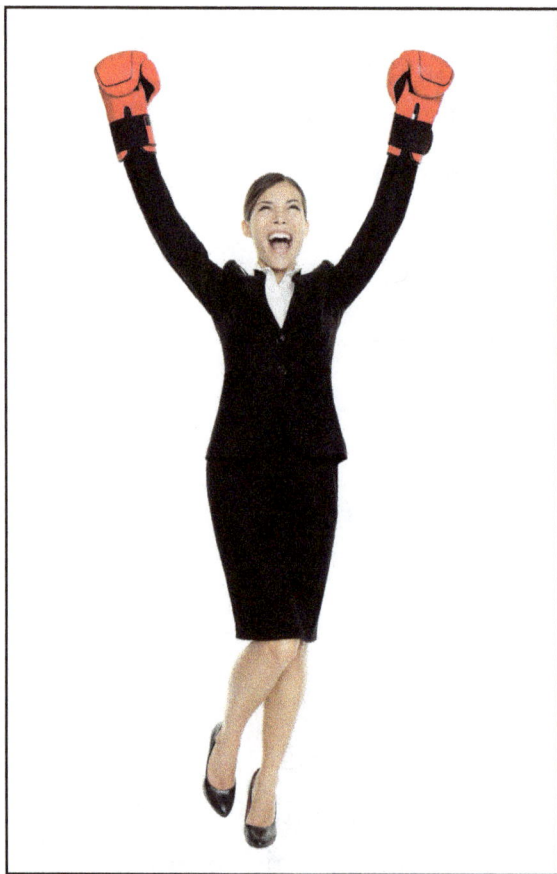

Share the AHA messages from this book socially by going to
http://aha.pub/GutsyLeaders.

Section II

Gutsy Leaders

Gutsy Leaders are ones who stand up for their beliefs even when it gets hard, which it does—a lot. That's how we grow. This section's messages help you learn about a few things to make you a Gutsy Leader.

35

Sometimes it is the quiet voice that gets heard, and #GutsyLeaders know how to use their range. @Pat_Obuchowski

_____

_____

_____

36

People are waiting for #GutsyLeaders to lead the way. @Pat_Obuchowski

_____

_____

_____

37

Don't give up on what you really want to do.
People wait for #GutsyLeaders to help them
do what they want to do. @Pat_Obuchowski

_____

_____

_____

38

#GutsyLeaders measure their true
successes by their fulfillment, happiness,
and relationships. @Pat_Obuchowski

_____

_____

_____

39

#GutsyLeaders are always starting
something -- even if it's to stop something.
@Pat_Obuchowski

_____

_____

_____

40

#GutsyLeaders notice their impact, as
they know others are noticing too.
@Pat_Obuchowski

_____

_____

_____

41

Stop arguing about who gets the crumbs.
#GutsyLeaders just make a bigger pie.
@Pat_Obuchowski

_____

_____

_____

42

#GutsyLeaders know their strengths and
make sure others know them too.
@Pat_Obuchowski

_____

_____

_____

43

#GutsyLeaders know their limitations, as
they know others know them too.
@Pat_Obuchowski

_____

_____

_____

44

#GutsyLeaders never commit their time
to things they aren't committed to.
@Pat_Obuchowski

_____

_____

_____

45

Being remarkable and being worth
someone remarking about is a goal of
#GutsyLeaders. @Pat_Obuchowski

_____

_____

_____

46

#GutsyLeaders know they are possibly a role model to someone. They strive to be the best one they can be.
@Pat_Obuchowski

_____

_____

_____

47

If they're not leading by example, #GutsyLeaders know they are not truly leading. @Pat_Obuchowski

_____

_____

_____

48

A #GutsyLeader does what they promised. @Pat_Obuchowski

_____

_____

_____

49

#GutsyLeaders are real. They make it safe for others to be real too. @Pat_Obuchowski

_____

_____

_____

50

#GutsyLeaders promise only those things they can deliver. Even to themselves. @Pat_Obuchowski

_____

_____

_____

51

When #GutsyLeaders have a vision, their work begins. @Pat_Obuchowski

_____

_____

_____

52

Listening is not a skill #GutsyLeaders ever multitask. @Pat_Obuchowski

_____

_____

_____

53

When needed, #GutsyLeaders stop the talking and start the walking. @Pat_Obuchowski

_____

_____

_____

Share the AHA messages from this book socially by going to
http://aha.pub/GutsyLeaders.

Section III

Building Other Gutsy Leaders: All about Your Team

If you want to make a difference, it can't be all about you. If your team shines, you shine. This section will help you realize the amazing and deep impact Gutsy Leadership has.

54

The way #GutsyLeaders are successful is by helping others do the same. @Pat_Obuchowski

_____

_____

_____

55

To get the best in people, #GutsyLeaders
expect the best in people.
@Pat_Obuchowski

_____

_____

_____

56

#GutsyLeaders coach the genius out of
others. @Pat_Obuchowski

_____

_____

_____

57

"Let go of what you know to learn from others" is a motto of #GutsyLeaders. @Pat_Obuchowski

_____

_____

_____

58

Since it's not what you get, it's what you
give, #GutsyLeaders give a lot.
@Pat_Obuchowski

_____

_____

_____

59

#GutsyLeaders give people the break they
wish someone had given to them.
@Pat_Obuchowski

_____

_____

_____

60

Engage others. Find allies. #GutsyLeaders know they don't need to do it by themselves. They know to ask others. @Pat_Obuchowski

_____

_____

_____

61

#GutsyLeaders stand by those who need them to. @Pat_Obuchowski

_____

_____

_____

Share the AHA messages from this book socially by going to
http://aha.pub/GutsyLeaders.

Section IV

Be Bold or Go Home

Gutsy Leadership is all about being bold. It is about leading with intention, passion, and determination. People follow leaders who inspire them with a great vision and great achievements. This section is about how a Gutsy Leader is not all about the "doing." It's also about the "being."

62

#GutsyLeaders know their truth and speak it. @Pat_Obuchowski

_____

_____

_____

63

#GutsyLeaders right wrongs. @Pat_Obuchowski

_____

_____

_____

64

At least one radical thing is done every day by #GutsyLeaders. @Pat_Obuchowski

_____

_____

_____

65

#GutsyLeaders start important things. @Pat_Obuchowski

_____

_____

_____

66

#GutsyLeaders live their life by choice, not chance. @Pat_Obuchowski

_____

_____

_____

67

"I don't know" is something #GutsyLeaders are wise enough to say. @Pat_Obuchowski

_____

_____

_____

68

Some reflect on the legacy they want to leave. #GutsyLeaders start living it. @Pat_Obuchowski

_____

_____

_____

69

#GutsyLeaders go as far as they can go to see what's there. Once there, they see enough to go further. @Pat_Obuchowski

_____

_____

_____

70

"Do something that scares me every day."
This is a saying of #GutsyLeaders.
@Pat_Obuchowski

_____

_____

_____

71

#GutsyLeaders make sure they remain
curious and ask the right questions.
@Pat_Obuchowski

72

Doing what pulls them rather than what
pushes them is what #GutsyLeaders do.
@Pat_Obuchowski

73

#GutsyLeaders rarely do things by
themselves. They always find allies.
@Pat_Obuchowski

_____

_____

_____

74

Double daring themselves is what
#GutsyLeaders do. @Pat_Obuchowski

_____

_____

_____

75

"What if success was easy?" is a question #GutsyLeaders ask themselves and then make success easy. @Pat_Obuchowski

_____

_____

_____

76

#GutsyLeaders look past the easy answers to find the right answers. @Pat_Obuchowski

_____

_____

_____

77

Sometimes in order to move forward, #GutsyLeaders know they must first retreat. @Pat_Obuchowski

_____

_____

_____

78

#GutsyLeaders are extraordinary ordinary people. @Pat_Obuchowski

_____

_____

_____

79

Experimenting as if the world's their playground is what #GutsyLeaders do, as they know the world IS their playground.
@Pat_Obuchowski

_____

_____

_____

80

If someone or something gets in their way, #GutsyLeaders simply walk around them.
@Pat_Obuchowski

_____

_____

_____

81

Righting wrongs is how #GutsyLeaders live their lives. @Pat_Obuchowski

----

82

Changing the convo from "What's wrong?" to "What needs to change to be better?" is what #GutsyLeaders ask themselves. @Pat_Obuchowski

----

83

One motto of #GutsyLeaders is, "Go Forth.
Do Good." @Pat_Obuchowski

_____

_____

_____

84

Instead of doing what they've always done, #GutsyLeaders choose to spark something new. @Pat_Obuchowski

_____

_____

_____

85

#GutsyLeaders make the world better by being better themselves and showing they care. @Pat_Obuchowski

_____

_____

_____

86

#GutsyLeaders do less and they do it better.
@Pat_Obuchowski

_____

_____

_____

87

#GutsyLeaders do the best they can and
assume others do too. @Pat_Obuchowski

_____

_____

_____

88

Little plans never inspire. That's why
#GutsyLeaders make big plans.
@Pat_Obuchowski

_____

_____

_____

89

"Yes" is easy to say. #GutsyLeaders learn to say "no" when it's needed.
@Pat_Obuchowski

_____

_____

_____

90

#GutsyLeaders bring their power to life.
@Pat_Obuchowski

_____

_____

_____

91

If what goes around comes around, #GutsyLeaders make the go around really great. @Pat_Obuchowski

_____

_____

_____

92

Since the view is quite breathtaking at the edge, that's where #GutsyLeaders take it to. @Pat_Obuchowski

_____

_____

_____

93

Do the thing you fear the most. #GutsyLeaders know if you do that one thing, you won't fear it any longer. @Pat_Obuchowski

_____

_____

_____

94

Why me? Why now? Why bother? Why
not? These are questions #GutsyLeaders
are always asking themselves.
@Pat_Obuchowski

_____

_____

_____

95

"Let's Get Gutsy and Get Going" -- a motto
for #GutsyLeaders to follow.
@Pat_Obuchowski

_____

_____

_____

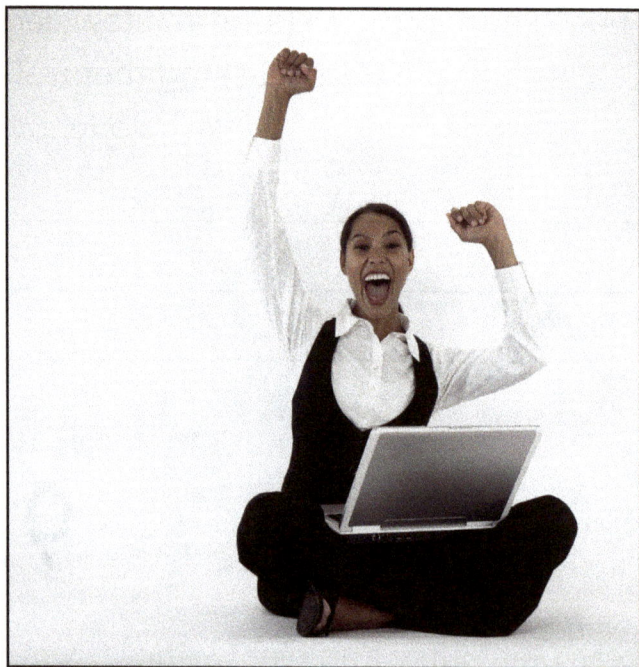

Share the AHA messages from this book socially by going to
http://aha.pub/GutsyLeaders.

Section V

Attitude Wins

Gutsy Leaders know they can change their attitude in a heartbeat and know how their attitude impacts everyone in their circle of influence. This section of AHAs reveals some ideas as to how to keep that attitude a positive one.

96

Adding, "Have some fun," to their
to-do list is what #GutsyLeaders do.
@Pat_Obuchowski

_____

_____

_____

97

#GutsyLeaders never apologize for who
they are. @Pat_Obuchowski

_____

_____

_____

98

#GutsyLeaders delight in their passions
and have them move their life forward.
@Pat_Obuchowski

_____

_____

_____

99

Change what you can. #GutsyLeaders
do this and then let go of what they can't
change. @Pat_Obuchowski

_____

_____

_____

100

Stop complaining. #GutsyLeaders know this is very unattractive. @Pat_Obuchowski

_____

_____

_____

101

Get it done and make it fun is what #GutsyLeaders know how to do really well. @Pat_Obuchowski

_____

_____

_____

102

Get great. It's never too late. #GutsyLeaders know this. @Pat_Obuchowski

_____

_____

_____

103

#GutsyLeaders make their livelihood lively.
@Pat_Obuchowski

_____

_____

_____

104

#GutsyLeaders know that the most radical act each of us can do in today's world is to be optimistic. @Pat_Obuchowski

_____

_____

_____

105

To be a #GutsyLeader, choose to be open and be ready. @Pat_Obuchowski

_____

_____

_____

106

It is okay not to know something and to admit it. #GutsyLeaders admit what they don't know. @Pat_Obuchowski

_____

_____

_____

107

#GutsyLeaders never linger in their doubts. @Pat_Obuchowski

_____

_____

_____

108

#GutsyLeaders surround themselves with inspiring people and are one themselves. @Pat_Obuchowski

_____

_____

_____

109

A #GutsyLeader motto: "Be good and if not, be great." @Pat_Obuchowski

_____

_____

_____

110

Be the bigger person. #GutsyLeaders know
when they are, and they help others be
bigger people too. @Pat_Obuchowski

_____

_____

_____

111

#GutsyLeaders get it done. Celebrate. Move
on. Repeat. @Pat_Obuchowski

_____

_____

_____

112

Go within. #GutsyLeaders look where they can matter, go within to find it, and then shout about it! @Pat_Obuchowski

_____

_____

_____

113

Enjoy the process, not just the results. #GutsyLeaders find what's juiciest in the process. @Pat_Obuchowski

---

114

#GutsyLeaders go right through life's red lights and proceed with passion. @Pat_Obuchowski

---

115

#GutsyLeaders are authentic. They know
if they are not; people will know.
@Pat_Obuchowski

_____

_____

_____

116

Let go of the idea that you can control the
outcome. #GutsyLeaders know they don't
control the outcome of anything.
@Pat_Obuchowski

_____

_____

_____

117

#GutsyLeaders have the expectation that
something great is about to happen and
they're going to be a part of it.
@Pat_Obuchowski

_____

_____

_____

118

#GutsyLeaders never invent problems that don't exist. @Pat_Obuchowski

_____

_____

_____

119

A #GutsyLeader plans their attitude for the positive. @Pat_Obuchowski

_____

_____

_____

120

Stay present to what's in front of you. #GutsyLeaders know the present is all they have. @Pat_Obuchowski

_____

_____

_____

121

#GutsyLeaders tip very well. Money and words. @Pat_Obuchowski

_____

_____

_____

122

#GutsyLeaders resolve to evolve.
@Pat_Obuchowski

_____

_____

_____

123

As much as #GutsyLeaders may fear
change, they fear not changing more.
@Pat_Obuchowski

_____

_____

_____

124

Stop saying, "I can't." #GutsyLeaders know they really mean, "I choose not to." And they say it. @Pat_Obuchowski

_____

_____

_____

125

Be a kind person to work with. All #GutsyLeaders we remember fondly are. @Pat_Obuchowski

_____

_____

_____

126

Show someone who really needs it a bit of kindness. #GutsyLeaders do. @Pat_Obuchowski

_____

_____

_____

127

In all dealings, #GutsyLeaders remember that a person's greatest emotional need is to be appreciated. @Pat_Obuchowski

_____

_____

_____

128

Get it over, then get over it, is an action
#GutsyLeaders take in difficult situations.
@Pat_Obuchowski

_____

_____

_____

Share the AHA messages from this book socially by going to
http://aha.pub/GutsyLeaders.

Section VI

Something Bigger Than You

Gutsy Leadership needs to be about something bigger than you. It is the legacy you are leaving. It is the difference you are making in your world, whether your family, neighborhood, church, office, city, state, and yes, even the entire world. This section of AHAs will aid you in looking outside yourself to the world you are impacting every day.

129

#GutsyLeaders find a way to help people feel good about themselves.
@Pat_Obuchowski

_____

_____

_____

130

Be inspired to aspire to be a #GutsyLeader.
@Pat_Obuchowski

_____

_____

_____

131

#GutsyLeaders live their lives with greater reverence. @Pat_Obuchowski

_____

_____

_____

132

"Who will my teacher be today?" is a question #GutsyLeaders ask themselves in their search for constant learning. @Pat_Obuchowski

_____

_____

_____

133

#GutsyLeaders work at what matters so they can matter. @Pat_Obuchowski

_____

_____

_____

134

Let yourself be touched by beauty today. #GutsyLeaders see the beauty all around them. @Pat_Obuchowski

_____

_____

_____

135

Make someone's day today. #GutsyLeaders
do this and are also gracious enough
to let someone make their day.
@Pat_Obuchowski

_____

_____

_____

136

"Do one thing to make it better." Regardless
of what that "it" is, #GutsyLeaders are always
making it better. @Pat_Obuchowski

_____

_____

_____

137

Looking for a different perspective? #Gutsy Leaders do this by changing their seat at the table. @Pat_Obuchowski

_____

_____

_____

138

A #GutsyLeader makes themselves
valuable. @Pat_Obuchowski

_____

_____

_____

139

Do the thing you fear most. If nothing else,
at least you won't fear it most any longer.
#GutsyLeaders do this. @Pat_Obuchowski

_____

_____

_____

140

Some of the best conversations we have
are the ones without words. #GutsyLeaders
practice this. @Pat_Obuchowski

_____

_____

_____

About the Author

Pat Obuchowski, an International Coach Federation (ICF) credentialed and certified coach, is the CEO (Chief Empowerment Officer) of inVisionaria (inVisionaria.com), an executive leadership and team development and coaching organization. She helps her clients go from good to great by sharpening their leadership, interpersonal, communication, and organizational skills, which help them achieve their vision on a professional and personal level.

Pat has worked with individuals and teams at for-profit organizations, such as McKesson, Cisco, Union Bank, and Lockheed, and nonprofit organizations, such as Kaiser Permanente, FUSE Corps, American Red Cross, and National Speaker's Association. She served as a Principal and Leadership Development Partner and coach with Pacific Gas & Electric Company, where she coached corporate leaders and teams to be more impactful in their work and in the world and helped them vision and play their Bigger Games.

Pat helps leaders build strong and results-oriented teams by mastering their strengths, managing their weaknesses, and becoming skillful in coaching others. She helps people create plans that inspire them and then coaches them in the implementation of those plans. She is also a public speaker, blogger, and the author of *Gutsy Women Win: How to Get Gutsy and Get Going* (GutsyWomenWin.com) and the co-author of *Scrappy Women in Business: Living Proof That Bending the Rules Isn't Breaking the Law.*

Pat is a contributor on Forbes Coaches Council and shares her leadership coaching ethos on Forbes.com (http://forbes.com/).

For more information: https://www.linkedin.com/in/patobuchowski/.

Contact Pat directly at Pat@inVisionaria.com.

An Invitation to Get Gutsy and Get Going

It's time get into action: to Get Gutsy and Get Going. Right here, right now. No backing out. I invite you to check out the website: www.GutsyWomenWin.com.

Come join us on:

Twitter @GutsyWomenWin

Facebook.com/GutsyWomenWin/

instagram.com/gutsywomenwin/

linkedin.com/in/patobuchowski

I invite you to contact me with any comments, atta-girls, input on what you need or are doing to Get Gutsy and Get Going, and about becoming a Gutsy Leader: Pat@GutsyWomenWin.com.

And most of all, I invite you to simply Get Gutsy and Get Going.

The world is waiting just for you.

AHAthat™

AHAthat makes it easy to share, author, and promote content. There are over 40,000 quotes (AHAmessages™) by thought leaders from around the world that you can share in seconds for free.

For those who want to author their own book, we have time-tested proven processes that allow you to write your AHAbook™ of 140 digestible, bite-sized morsels in eight hours or less. Once your content is on AHAthat, you have a customized link that you can use to have your fans/advocates share your content and help grow your network.

➲ Start sharing: http://AHAthat.com

➲ Start authoring: http://AHAthat.com/Author

Hey, Did You AHAthat™?
Pat Obuchowski
AHAthat Author

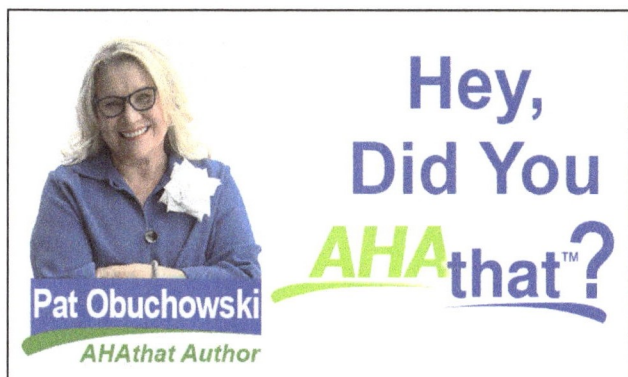

Please go directly to this book in AHAthat and share each AHAmessage socially at
http://aha.pub/GutsyLeaders